NO TIME FOR DEATH

Harris Gardner

Červená Barva Press
Somerville, Massachusetts

Červená Barva Press
P.O. Box 440357
W. Somerville, MA 02144-3222

www.cervenabarvapress.com

Bookstore: www.thelostbookshelf.com

Cover Art: "Carmencita" by William Merritt Chase (1890)

Cover design: William J. Kelle

ISBN: 978-1-950063-59-8

Library of Congress Control Number: 2021950808

ACKNOWLEDGMENTS

The author would like to thank the editors of the following journals in which these poems have appeared:

The Aurorean: "Among Us"
Bagels with the Bards # 1, #7, # 10: "Almost a Poet," "Butt," "Name Tags"
Chest: "So, You Want To Be in Films"
Concrete Wolf: "Sneak Peek at a Poet's Will"
Constellations: "Peak of Promise"
Cool Plums: " Landlubber"
Endicott Review: "Spin Cycle"
Fulcrum #6: "Stop Watch"
Harvard Review: "Che Sera May Be," "Comma"
Ibbetson Street: #32, #33, #35, #36, #37, #39, #45: "In the Loo," "Spirit in A Bottle," "Paradigm," "In a Spot," "Hold It," "Lassitude," "Mark Your Fear of the Dark"
Jewish Advocate: "Barbed Wire"
Main Street Rag: "Until the Last Recorded Dime"
Midstream: "Cemetery Visit"
Muddy River Poetry Review: "Will and Witness"
The New Renaissance: "Sheepskin"
A Poet's Siddur: "Softer Than Silence"
Rosebud: "Landlubber"
Vallum: (Canada): "I-F"
Wilderness House Literary Review.com: "Among Us"

"Barbed Wire" also appeared in *I Refused to Die: A Holocaust Study* by Susie Davidson.

Special thanks to the following: my long time muse and dear friend, Lainie Senechal, Rhina P. Espaillat, "Empress of the poetry universe," Gloria Mindock/ Červená Barva Press, my publisher with the patience of a saint and for her supreme faith in this collection. Bill Kelle, for his technical "magic" on the manuscript. Kathleen Spivack, for her professional observations on many of these poems, to my siblings, Brenda Gardner and Dr. Allan Gardner for their familial support and encouragement, and my sister-in-law Barbara Gardner; Joanna Nealon for her keen ear and comments, George Kalogeris, for his belief in this collection, Fred Marchant and Jennifer Barber with admiration and thanks, a special shout out to Doug Holder and all the Bagel Bards, to my late mother, Elaine Zelman Gardner Prober, for her life-long appreciation for my poetry, to my late father, Dr. Abraham Gardner, and a special thanks to my Rabbi, Elizabeth Stern, Dr. Cynthia Marturano, my primary physician for closely monitoring my health issues, and to my cousins Barbara Scolnick, Ben Bachrach, Elizabeth Bachrach–Tan, Robert Bachrach and their spouses for their enthusiasm for my poetry.

TABLE OF CONTENTS

An Argument with Time

Contemplating Mortality Instead of My Navel

Negotiating for an Afterlife

INTRODUCTION

If you're a reader who enjoys language that invites you into an experience instead of simply describing it, who likes action verbs that make events real, who delights in the surprise phrase that seems surreal at first but then, on second thought, feels just right, this book is for you.

Its title tells you at once that Harris Gardner, well-known New England poet and literary activist, is ready to challenge the inevitable. But the titles to its three subsections add that this struggle will be no mere, common verbal fistfight, but rather a cunning diplomatic affair requiring more mind and music than muscle. The poems are mostly free verse, but constructed with every device in the formal poet's toolbox: rhyme—both end and internal—and rhythm; alliteration, puns, repetition and every other game to please the ear; similes, direct address, personification of odd abstractions, and witty extended metaphors.

All this playfulness turns up both in open form poems and in villanelles, list poems and occasionally-disguised sonnets, along with ingenious references to the work of poets living and dead, including Eliot, Kipling, Whittier, Longfellow and Williams, as well as the Bible, mythology and popular song.

Gardner often uses a title to frame a poem in a situation that works like the premise of a joke. For instance, in a poem titled "So You Want to Be in Films" he introduces the theme of failing health and the many state-of-the-arts available now that acquaint us with our internal organs. A poem about time as we live it includes the haunting phrase, "The future, a bruised suitcase/ On the carousel of baggage claims." "Sneak Peek at the Poet's Will" ends with a startling echo of the Lord's Prayer," and another poem describes the shameless advances of a clingy, annoying, needy would-be girlfriend who persists in stalking him everywhere, despite his rebuffs.

And at the end, when we think we know what he's up to, Gardner surprises us by taking a subtle unexpected turn I won't spoil by revealing it. Read the book instead and discover it for yourself!

Rhina P. Espaillat
Author of *The Field* and co-author with Alfred Nicol of *An Accident of Light: Poems of Newburyport*

NO TIME FOR DEATH

An Argument with Time

Stop Watch

Let's start by shredding all the odd years.
Then, take a match to all the evens.
Slice and dice all the minutes until they bleed white.
Pound in a block to slow the growling gears.
Mortar and pestle the grinding seconds. Blunt their bite.
Smash all the clocks, yes, the craven cuckoos, too.

Fast-forwarding the film frames few regrets, though
The mirror shows the sweep-hand rounding your face.
There is no crystal case to hold your works.
It's not time's business to offer you perks.
The crushing R.I.P. tide crinkles your crown.
Worn out, you may drown, still, in the shallows.

Your mind stores snapshots, both fuzzy and clear.
Photo albums freeze mortality's stare.
The lens is keen. It sees what it sees.
The present deep cleans an encrusted past;
Then polishes it to a pristine sheen.
Future scenes, left alone, develop on their own.

Pare away the wrinkled pages.
Strip bare temporal confusion.
Vanity's illusion brooms the dust.
Search the phases of your soul.
Find the last clock. Make it whole.
When the keeper sleeps, he loosens control.

Che Sera May Be

The best period of my life was / is, was / is, was / is.
My thoughts meander beyond the horizon;
Detour back from dead-end streets.
Toes stub on rocks that poke up their heads
To see what stirs lazy layers of dust.
Feet bleed on thorns of decapitated roses.
Penance for the break-out, rampaging ideas
That refuse to return when called home for dinner.
Seeds drop into other gardens; grow organic groceries
For perhaps more deserving palates.

I will / won't recognize the best days ahead
Behind, or now as they saunter by
Dressed in top hats and tails, no, make that
Red checkered shirts, open collars and jeans.
Better attire to kneel on fresh turned land
And nurture what remains – solid food with a
Liberal sprinkle of spice, otherwise bland.
Che sera, may be. Have to get me some rope
And corral those doggies. No need to have them
Wander across some other pasture.

No Time for Death

Time counts down for all of us:
Ten, nine, eight... none appreciate
Its flight, the path of no return.
Too often, we do a slow burn on a short fuse.
A little fizzle, a stutter, then it's boom, baby.

Our ashes rain down on every abandoned plane
Called Nowhere. No time to complain, to prepare.
Not a moment left to reflect, to regret
"Our laying waste to all our powers."
Time is an arbitrary asset.

When we shatter the fragile hours,
Nothing remains in the bone-man's sack.
We cannot choose to refuse the invitation.
We can only walk the walk on the streets of the dead.
We can offer up prayers for life on some prefab plane
Where the CFO keeps the brittle book of our days.

Maybe the weights will balance in our favor.
Maybe we shall come back to clean up loose ends.
Maybe the sentence gets upended, gets suspended.
Seven, six five, four, three, two -
Will you stop for one forsaken minute!

Compass Overboard

Time's hands turn the vessel's wheel of chance.
Wind fills the bellies of ballooning sails.
Bubbles foam on frothy crest.
An uncorked bottle blesses the bow.

One moment the craft rides the swells;
Then, the depths stretch out their questing claws
And chant an ascending crescendo.
The sun bleeds its red omen into the ocean.

Indigo sky conspires with sudden gale
To change our cherished charts.
Strident sea drums on Cyclops' stones;
Threatens to strand the ship upon the dunes;
To wreck and scatter battered bones
On sands as bleak as beak-pierced eyes.

Will and Witness

I have tilted at the windmills of time
For the greater part of my fragile breath.
Death sits mounted, holds a poised lance
To challenge to a game of chance I cannot win.

Though I go ten rounds, and still ten, again,
Though the referee may deem it a draw;
Though I dance and weave around the ring,
Death will sound the knell for a TKO.

A stealthy shaft in the shoulder
Or a toothy twinge in the knee
Warns that I should devise a will.
There is still the won't of denial.

Perhaps, let them make a well-stoked pyre.
My body will briefly feed the flowering flames.
Then, let the wind take my powdered remains
To sate the salivating maw of the sea.

My sanity grows wings, becomes suspect.
I appoint God to be both expert witness
And executor of my final designs.
He may choose first from my lean legacy.

The wattage of my inner light wages with the wind.
Heaven may take me on a simple whim.
My knickknacks and baubles left behind
Go to those who wish to reap an odd keepsake.

The will, though strong, bends like a willow.
I prepare to submit to the terminal triumph.
My pen is poised to write a sole codicil.
I am content to contemplate my ashes.

Inconvenient Baggage

The was was awhile ago.
It was not a happy was
Because no one wanted
To be taught by was. They thought
Will be, a promise, more or less.

Was was neglected, abused.
First drafts, tomes, and bridges
Fueled bonfires. Fuming was for naught.
These postcards for posterity
Were a banquet for flames.

Was became hoarse from shouts,
Diatribes, vain endeavors
To connect the end with less-than-perfect
Beginnings. Was rattled and lurched to mute.
The embers of was reduced heating bills.

Left over words became prophecy.
Was stuck in third gear;
Now is a stop light.
The future, a bruised suitcase
On the carousel in baggage claims.

What Memories We Bring to Middle Age

What memories we bring to middle age.
Mistakes of youth we wish we could forget.
Life might be better as an empty page.

Foolish youth learns little from the stage.
Mothers, fathers can only smile or fret.
What memories we bring to middle age.

Changes in adolescence made us rage
At efforts to ensnare in form or net.
Life might be better as an empty page.

How bland our lives would be if seen in beige.
We learn wisdom from our books or sweat.
What memories we bring to middle age.

We play at freedom in an open cage;
The legacy of might-have-been leaves debt.
Life might be better as an empty page.

The value of rewards is hard to gauge
When viewed in light of hindsight and regret.
What memories we bring to middle age.
Life might be better as an empty page.

Lassitude

My metronome rocking chair keeps the measure
While I stare at the stain on the ceiling.
Time squeezes through a tiny fissure
Surrounded by peeling paint.
The minutes breeze out a window
Where they become a beautiful woman
Who walks around my edifice,
Waits patiently with her artifice.

I become a scholar. My eyes study
That spreading spot.
Perhaps I discover Noah in profile
Or the Madonna from a tub that overflowed;
Or God forbid, from a faulty toilet.
That Rorschach blot sings lullabies to my brain.
Time wearies of my absence and returns
To find her lover has gone musty with mildew.

While the instant art snares my mind,
Flames charcoal my dinner.
Somewhere, tongues lick a building's bones;
Then, sirens voices vex no more.
Dogs and cats form discussion groups.
Soggy newspapers dissolve,
So I miss the comics, obits,
And that small, false alarm
Of my impending demise.

While I video the crumbling edges,
I avoid bills and other incendiary notes.
The wallpaper sloughs in a slow striptease.
I recall four canines playing poker.
Time returns in her curves
And satin sheath to call my bluff.

In the Loo

The medicine cabinet mirror
Bears your reflection
For pre-coffee inspection –
A meticulous search for lines
That mark hoary age.
Very few sleuthing clues
Stare back to discomfort you.

Soothing lather conceals your face;
Prepares the razor's track.
The first stroke makes a miniscule nick.
This produces a welling drop of blood,
Proof that you're no blue-blood.
You can wait for a blue moon;
But that won't change an urge to brood.

You complete your morning ablutions
While contemplating solutions.
You track stray strands of last night's
Picasso dream. Memory seems to shut
The door to recollection.
Vision, cleared of cobwebs,
Notes that white and gray dominate
Your shocks full crop.
The silent song spins.
Was yesterday so long ago?

Mortals with Spirits

"Time passed away"- Sophie Grimes

An E-vite landed in my e-mail from cyberspace.
My first fleeting thought was to delete it.
Unknown address suggested spam;
Perhaps a virus- Heaven forbid!

Morbid curiosity deposed the discreet.
Opened, concern turned to amazement.
The content stated, in a short announcement:
"We regret to advise you that Time passed away."
A wake is scheduled at Chapel of the Stars.
All sentiments are welcome."

No hour offered, just a date and directions
To a mesa in New Mexico; and a promise
Of a spirited event.
I don't know when I assented; but, arriving
There, I found standing room only –
Not even a seat in sight.

Attired in white linen finery,
Time reposed in open coffin.
His shorn locks were at an
Orderly shoulder length;
Former copious beard,
Scythed to a mere van dyke.

His visage evoked dried figs.
We stood still, silenced, stunned.
All had believed the myth
That Time was, well, timeless;
But there he was, serenely asleep.

We recalled the sundry junctures
When it was taken for granted.
In our youth, we little noted its flow,

Though we had boated daily on the river.
Now all seemed beyond retrieval.

We uncorked a few bottles, perhaps more
Than a few, which we consumed
Yes, in no time at all.
The throngs were in fine spirits.
We were ebullient.
Our eyes absorbed the stars.

We celebrated, swapped memories,
Resuscitated some long submerged.
The imbibing continued unabated.
A last bottle was decisively passed around.
Sound was sagely mitigated.
We paid our somber respects
To departed Time.

Nothing left to do but to drift
Back to our separate parts,
Known and not, somewhat sober –
Well, still a bit drunk, if you must know.
Bereft, tottering, we suffered Time to pass.

Paradigm

You lie in the swirling night
And tabulate swarms of stars.
Sometimes you sense that
Myriad sidereal flares
Burn their eternal flame.

You wonder whether it's simpler
To comprehend grains of ancient sand
Or immortal clusters that stream
Across bewildered vision.

The surf sorts scrubbed pebbles;
Arranges groups in mystical
Design: uneven rows and forms,
Remains of former majesty.

In the city's cemetery,
The stones are finite,
Indifferent to calm or storms.
Rampant tears will not wear them thin;
But keening wind and rain weigh down dolor.

Some, who sleep, have traveled past
The need to total sums of sheep.
Tides have rubbed against succumbing
Lives; and tumble water-logged dolls
Onto sea-honed sullen slabs.

You ponder what fires will consume
Profusion of human wicks.
Your mind surrounds profound measures.
You treasure metronome heartbeats
While unsolvable stars gleam
Your course into ephemeral dreams.

River Watch

Languid time propels
Fourteen canoes, each
With a crew of two.
There's no rush to arrive
Anywhere, but some young
Fools zig-zag across the path
Of steady human engines who
Paddle with persistent rhythm
On this three hour journey
Of profound discovery –

Past the roosting rare Great Egret,
Past the obsolete Waltham Watch factory.
We softly follow the river,
Parallel to a cemetery
Filled with harvested souls
Whose dreams and rest are rippled
By a lone coyote that converses
With the seasoned full moon.
The creature peppers the hushed dark
With barks and moans in solitude.

The small flotilla muscles along
Under the eyes of the silvered observer.
Regal paired swans maintain calm vigil
In distant reaches of their realm.
No crashing waves intrude
On this idyllic hot night
Tempered with a cool soothing breeze.
Whimsical sculptures peer through the trees:
A group of deer, an alligator, an iguana
On a lower branch, and an upright bear.
They will be there long after we disappear.

The third hour passes with recurrent cheer;
Yet, the clock draws us nearer to reality,
The subdued cacophony of the turnpike.
Memories hover; we revel in the receding
Camaraderie. The river reflects companion moon
That bids us adieu in rear-view mirror.

King Winter, Mother Spring

From Rorschach clouds,
A hand inscribes flowing words
That bleed from a sword-edged pen.
To the Winter King:
"Mene, mene, tekel upharsin"
"Your days are numbered;
You are found wanting."

The ice monarch bristles a menacing retort:
"Look upon my crystal walls,
My castles and frost-laden forts
That my blizzard breath erects.
All life born in my domain
I hold in perpetual thrall."

A voice that chimes with promise
Causes ice bricks to crack and fall.
Hoary turrets topple.
Slices of glassy slabs
Rumble down ramparts.

The Queen's nurturing song weaves
An array of hardy flowers-in-waiting.
Ice fangs melt into muddy pools.
A plethora of plants push
Above the pulsing ground.

Hibernal bones dissolve
As the sun stretches light.
Siberian tyrant sleeps
On a drift-buried bier.
Mother Spring marshals her army.
She holds sway in the realm, for now.

Beyond Life Support

An unfinished draft
Lies unmourned on a mound;
Abandoned at the town dump
Despite vows to Heaven
And yourself to see it through.
Winged scavengers keen their dirge.
Solo sorties target the corpse.

You shed no tears as they dive
To pluck an i or some other
Vowel; a choice phrase
Disappears; another tidbit
Of a line is a tasteless morsel
Gulped down a gull's gullet.

No feathered fiends pick at the guts.
There aren't any despite many rewrite efforts.
Perhaps it was the malformed heart
Or misshapen, shriveled lungs.
No extreme measures to resuscitate.

In a small candle length silence,
Remember the form that breathed.
It will restore a more vital poem
When it breaches an entrance into the world

Passing Go

No need to yield to true evidence
Of minutes' merciless march,
Though they continue to accrue.
Erect barriers to Time's seductive embrace.

Off-the-shelf one-a-days
And camouflage to conceal natural wrinkles
Push remedies to aid the white lie in the mirror:
The mirage of a young face.

The grandfather clock begs to differ,
Though some stand tall and walk
With a youthful gait after
A stripped hip was replaced.

Aggregate years grow weeds
That mingle in a lush garden.
Despite our best defense, time observes
No stop signs. We endure another lap
In the race to advance to go.

Until the Last Recorded Dime

When you have been broke a very long time,
You forego the champagne, but not the beer.
Such is life when you live from dime to dime.

Ears are deaf to complaint, you play the mime.
You look in the mirror and face down fear
When you have been broke a very long time.

You must defer to your reason and rhyme;
To make the ascent, you shift to first gear.
It's never easy, life, from dime to dime.

You can't stop the hands, the clock tolls the chime,
So you grin and concoct a mask of cheer
When you have been broke a very long time.

Your efforts ease you into the sublime.
You move to the beat only you can hear.
You adapt when you live from dime to dime.

Each day you wash away more of the grime.
Your mind is full, but your focus is clear.
You manage to manage after a time.
No more holding your breath from dime to dime.

Pass This Way Another Day

I set my watch twenty minutes fast
To be consistent with my rounds;
Perhaps, too, it may confuse the chauffeur
Who cruises in the black limousine.
He makes a u-turn to double check
Addresses and his infernal calendar.

I peek out behind half-closed blinds.
My "shoo, shoo" is a charm against the day
When my clock's battery runs down.
The cuckoo dreams in black and white;
Flecks peel from its painted body.

I sip my mango margarita, savor every drop;
Celebrate life for yet another summer.
Perhaps sunglasses help my youthful disguise.
Hopefully, my fate is not a chiseled date.
No rush, I can wait even if I'm late.
Pass by Dark Harvester. Do what you must;
But, as for me, just pass.

Almost a Poet

Once upon a clock
In a wound down time,
An hour starved to shadow
Nibbled and nicked by
Razor seconds that flowed
Through a slit in its fabric.

A bullet built a nest
In a young soldier's brain.
A youth so certain of forever.
Only the old volunteered
Lead foot brakes that called
Halt to breath.

Death's surprise etched his eyes.
Strange to find a wild flower
Field to nevermore.
In his mud-caked pocket,
Medics found half-finished poems,

Verses penned in a dim light's halo.
No closure, no end unless
A home flared the window
Of a soul with compass wings
To dress new stanzas in bone and flesh.

Mark Your Fear of the Dark

I am scared that when my number is called,
It won't be in the supermarket checkout lane.
I am scared that I won't be prepared
When my final sum is tabulated.
My mind needs a proper house keeping
To clean up the clutter from the stored mundane.
I am scared that my lack
Of mental acuity results from
The countdown of my allotted hours.

I am scared to ponder the loss of powers
Of my body parts, particularly my heart and brain.
Twice a year I shall not fear the shrinking list of ills,
Perhaps imaginary, from which I refuse the profuse
Placebos or a lexicon of suggested pills.
The semi-annual visits to a polished physician
Is my interim solution to personal confession.
I am still scared that the light at tunnel's end
Is more than the brightness of my yearly MRI.

If I properly prepare, I shall not fear the shadow
Of a scythe on my living room wall. It may be
Nothing at all-only a first cousin to the remnants
Of a Rorschach blot. If I tend to diurnal chores,
That are all parcels of a well-told story,
I shall not fear the final mystery's form.

A Song for Humankind

Now, the scent of hope's perfume
Permeates a land formerly afflicted
By a steady drip of sheer despair.
Feeble light had flickered in noisome gloom.

Ominous clouds had augured ill
For the lingering life of liberty.
Then, sunburst's sword sliced
Through nightmare's twisted knot
That was throttling freedom's voice.

Now, the tyrant's impaired statues
That tottered on crumbling foundations
Topple to resounding ovations.
Nothing remains except defaced heads

That once commanded multitudes
To gaze upon his works with awe
And masked dismay. Now, these
Artifacts are displayed to jocund jeers.

Where once a country was sinking
Into a fog of loathing and fear,
Now throngs are poised to proceed
In parades of joyful song.
Altogether, a great, new day

Of elation and celebration
Is pealing the harmony of promise.
So, sing a song of brotherhood
And sisterhood, a song for humankind.

Contemplating Mortality Instead of My Navel

So, You Want To Be in Films

Act One, scene One, take One.
A genetic aberration:
Hypertrophic cardiomyopath
I can't even pronounce it.

My heart has become a star.
Hello, Hollywood, good-by.
My pulsing muscle stays here with me.
I can't bear to be apart from it.

The MRI- The camera covers all
The angles: close-ups and long shots.
My heart is a ham. It performs
An unscripted dance.

A cocoon immerses me in Mozart's music.
A tunnel floods with light;
Still, I want to dream.

The technician keeps me alert.
"Breathe, exhale, hold your breath."
I am drowning in light.

Film flashes forward.
Visit to the Cardiologist,
An exchange of jests.
"About the murmur,
What's it saying?"

Then, a picture chart
Explains the challenges
To monitor the murmured refrain.
A new take on the "Tell-Tale Heart."

Asymptomatic-no pain or related
Symptoms. No end credits to roll.
Then, the piece de resistance:
The specialist flips a switch.

There it is, stage-center,
The star! The doctor shows the area
Of the third rail: moderate aortic stenosis.
Case not closed.

Not a five star rating?
Edgy, no holds barred.
Thoughtful, provoking!
More than a life-time.
Of performances.
No beta-blockers, yet!

No edited film.
No cutting board projected.
For now, the heart-frets are "minor".
Later is a distant day.

This is a wrap!

Balancing Act

Seven, six, five, four, three, two,
For Heaven's Sake! I am still awake.
The crew programs their craft for on-cue hues.
High-tech intones the ritual review:
Microscope, check, lens implant, all-clear.
The stage is set, bright lights in place.
It's a sunny morning in Cataract City.

Who cares how long it takes?
Forty minutes feel like five.
This is live T.V., no canned applause.
Pilot to automatic pilot
Wake me when we touch down.
Are we there yet? Almost done?

The team is in stitches.
None for me, in the right eye.
Had two when they re-tooled the left one.
They try to slow my monologue;
My tongue is in hyper-drive.
What's in the intravenous, anyway?
I see the light, it is good.

In the first life-altering event,
I snoozed through the entire show,
New vision in a blink.
This time, it's opening night.
The pair are balanced, astounding sight!
I'm looking great, no miscues.
Pass around the Corona cigars.
Praise the Lord! My eyes are reborn.

Sisyphus in Recovery

Which stone did roll up
The steep, craggy slope?
I don't actually remember.
It may have been one of the
First two that passed enroute
To the emergency room.

More likely, it was the sole "boulder",
Embedded, immune to frantic complaints.
Why it was sent to subject me
To spiraling pain, I can't explain
That enigma. Was it seized from a past
Life; the continuing karma
Of a mythical ancestor?

Another view-genetic flaw.
Why was my system in revolt?
Charts and monitoring machines
Ran rapid commentary.
The questions that remain
Are beyond the physical plane.

A paltry two percent,
Destined for normal recovery,
Is the standard prognosis when
Tormenting stones disrupt body
And alleged Soul. For over half,
It is ordained, no hope.

Perhaps the stone was a warning
To atone, to pay more attention
To the intangible. I passed
In and out of life sans memory
Of these worrisome passages.

Vital re-intubation became a dilemma.
A serene senior physician
Secured my corporeal salvation;
He re-inserted the tube of breath and life.

I floated between two worlds.
As the third day waned, I awoke.
I slowly rediscovered myself.
No shining light, but there was illumination.
No antecedents faded back to that other world.

The rough stone was removed
From my near-death adventure.
It remains balefully balanced
On the barren peak's verge.
For now, life surges; that is enough.

Addiction

It does not seem to be a sound solution
To make a New Year's resolution
To cure my aggravating, albatross addiction.
It may be a rather facile prediction
That sweets will determine my termination
On my tootsie pop terra firma.

Hello, I am - who are you? My anonymous
Name tag boldly declares me to be a chocaholic.
I have paced and retraced the twelve exact steps
To the kitchen cabinet where the cocoa treats are stored.
My affliction is ironic like being gored by a bull
In a colorful candy kiosk.

Mounds of mint girl scout cookies have mounted a retreat.
I am beginning to tremble like a milkshake in a blender.
I grope for the last bar of Godiva - gone! My barren
Cupboard mocks me. Chocolate chips were preemptively
Chucked into a forgotten waste bin.

Brownies have staged their last stand. No crumbs, even
To sustain a mouse. The final tinseled kiss slid down
The chute of my tongue. Its echoed sigh resounded
In its ultimate melt-down. And, Lord protect me from
The temptation of siren Reeces Pieces.

Shall I venture, then, to make a visit,
In my voracious quest, to the convenience store?
Maybe just a pint of fudge swirl ice cream-
My chocolate dreams are becoming nightmares!
Dare I go and dare I go cold turkey? That should be

The golden key to my guided future recovery.
Perhaps, now, just a wee flute of chocolate liqueur.
This year, I resolve to indulge no more
In my Holy Grail pursuit of face-your-demons chocolate
Even if, to the sound of sacred music, the ultimate
Hot fudge sundae should rise from the deepest, heated pit.

Message for the Bees
(With Apologies to J.G. Whittier)

As soon as winter bleats its last,
I plan to put a pinch of spring breeze
In my nose to hasten the new green season.
Any subsequent sneezing fits will help the bees
Pursue their pollinating labor.

Meanwhile, their queen fills the hive
With a thriving industry of future drones.
Soon, her strength will be on the wane.
Maybe someone should tell the bees
That eternity calls for youth to carry on
The royal task. Nobody asked me;

It's not my job to advise them.
With my luck, I would need to dart away
From an angry diving swarm.
Stung once, shame on me.
Stung twice, shame on you.
Stung more than that, call me

An ambulance. I shall be prone
From flailing and choreographing avoidance.
Allergy, what allergy? I've been pierced before.
The hives are alive with the buzz
Of the bees' soporific music.

If I could set clock hands for spring,
And ring in early flowers
With the cooperating alarm,
Such magic might defeat all other charms;
But no, the snow paints transient scenes on window panes.
I must endure winter's prevailing pain.
Spring will come. If I survive, I shall inform the bees.

*"Telling the Bees"- John Greenleaf Whittier- Also a nineteenth century practice, when someone died, the bee hives would be covered to keep the bees from leaving, before telling the bees of the owner's demise.

Mourn the Monarch

No one prescribed this diet.
It is not a matter of weight.
This shouts for survival of fruited plains.
Amber waves of grain are genetically
Honed. Altered states of corn
Are committing regicide to orange brilliance
Blended with widow's exquisite lace.

We are woven into the tapestry.
When you warp the frayed food chain,
What will remain on moribund menu?
Meat? No, no! Hormonally enhanced.
Most milk? Harmful to your health.
Tomatoes? Same problem as beef.
Ninety-five percent of soy struggles for identity.
You don't want to know about potatoes!
Jelly-fish genes to make the harvest iridescent
For magnificent moisture control?

The white coats are coming!
The white coats are coming!
Sound the clarion from highest cliffs.
Land of our birth is bloated
With full mutant bread baskets.
Bio-tech savants are force-feeding the masses.
"So, you don't like the food."
"We have ways to make you eat it."
"Where does it say, use caution
With these ingredients?"

What effect on pregnant earth?
Milkweed wings fold forever.
Fingers bleed as grip slips;
A bit of membrane lingers.
Strands drift while bones sleep.
Most butterflies are free;
But the monarchs are dying!

Tapestry at Joppa Flats

A small flock of plovers
Settles onto Joppa Flats.
They mingle with sandpipers,
Yellow legs, dowitchers, and gulls,
Harmoniously foraging
For disparate fare.

A great egret sails by slowly
On its own quest for sustenance.
An osprey circles on overhead currents.
Keen eyes seek a hapless fish
Whose lack of quick flight
Renders an escape route moot.

Binoculars pivot to capture
This aviary tableau,
Vibrant scenery similarly suited
For a wallpaper motif
In halcyon homes that celebrate
Year-round ocean panorama.

Sea breeze and cloud shade
Alleviate the sun's protracted heat.
The patient hawk plunges in sudden descent.
Talons pierce ill-fated prey in relentless grasp.
Final drama: fins surrender in ironic gasp
Of too much air. Fabric's ripples disappear.

Echoes of Frost

Roots run deep on the lawn
Near the edge of the lake.
Leaves flutter, small anchored butterflies
That bob on the breeze that fills moored sails.

Storms roll down Merrimack valley,
Wrestle limbs that now droop with fatigue.
Maybe these arms once held youth
That scrambled toward the top for sport;
Boys that knew not to fly too near the sun.

In the fall, reluctant feet troop
Toward the chalkboard prison of books
Where stolen glances observe birds
Learning their survival lessons.
The birches, left behind, whisper memories.

Washing Potatoes

Scrub the clean soil from the surface.
Scrape carefully, no nicks to mix your blood.
Section fruit of the earth's womb.
Next, the grater creates pulpy essence.
Onion layers peel back memories
That ducts cleanse and sanitize.
The sizzle in the skillet
Teases the taste.

Today, I rinse the skins,
Prepare them for baking.
Traditions fade with calendar pages.
Now, mother wears her age
Like wrinkled fries.
Her face and mind retain their spark;
Aching joints only half respond
To therapeutic heat.
She frets and tabulates the minutes
While toiling stove completes the task.

Sneak Peek at a Poet's Will

Item: Verses nurtured
On marrow from
Singing bones,
Under layers of dust

Item: Stanzas dressed in flesh
From the heart, draped in
Surplus brain pulsations,
Wrapped in packet
With blood-red ribbon

Item: Excess of bottled tears
Sprinkles pavement;
Grows roses that bite
When one stops to inhale.

Item: Lines borrowed or stolen,
Nudge blank mind in bold directions.
Serve fresh on special occasions.
Bury stale thoughts, separately.

Item: Crumpled bag, home to
A few nibbled on metaphors.
Most emotions spent,
Some wisely,
Relish the remnants.

Item: The desk that birthed
Over-burdened pages
Can be left to no one.

It labors without complaint
When images gallop off the paper
Become ingrained in splinters and stains
The legs wobble speak with creaks
Untranslated versions.

Item: Voices of verses,
        Captured with accurate tone.
        Napkins and other inspired fragments
        Thrown in drawers, for the moment.

        This is not the final statement.
        Premature to lament
        Unwritten passions.
        Volumes will increase,
        Collections bound.
        The will will be done.

Sheepskin

Perhaps you sit in an inspired moment.
Maybe your neck hairs prickle
At a peculiar presence
As you pen metered lines
Onto blank parchment
Of a fine grained hand-made writer's book.

Nothing angelic or demonic—
Try a stretch, perhaps a sheep shade
Freshly escaped from Eternity's pasture,
Peers over your shoulder, perplexed
At symbols it cannot understand .

You don't hear its silent bleats
And laments as it stomps invisible feet
When it discovers an apparent answer
In the current use of its original skin.

Undisturbed, you listen
To the poem's heartbeat
As you shape its life and craft its form.
You pray, as the dumb beast might have,
Had it been able, to escape the butcher's blade,
And you, the slaughterhouse critics.

Comma

"A woman once said to Flaubert, I wrote
Twenty thousand words today. What did you do?
Flaubert replied I removed the comma that I put in last week."

A comma tiptoes into all our lives.
We pause as we pursue our sentence.
No comma burrows within the bones.
A comma constricts the breath
When winter's hand grips the throat.
A comma fish hooks your gut
When the burden snags you in the net.
A comma slow motions your dreams
That drip through intravenous tubes.
A comma gnaws through the ropes after death.
The voice of the bell peals, then pauses.

Vanishing Point

I want to say that this is the one
Hour that I am cautiously content;
Then a question mark hovers overhead,
An inverted hook. Will I nibble the bait?

I wonder, instead, about the when
Of my elastic happy moment that snaps
If it stretches ecstatically far.

Did it really reside in the not-so-visible past,
Or is it yet to arrive, a visitor
From an unfettered future
That harbors a heaven of curtained dreams?

What star misses my wistful wish
So that it becomes a mere eyelash
On the moon's puckish face?

I want to trek through this flowering hour,
Eternity's spec of silica that streams unchecked.
I want to follow the beckoning hand.
Where it vanishes, I shall explore an ageless land

Landlubber

The Seven Voyages of Sinbad,
A movie viewed almost fifty years ago.
Memory hoists its sails on an ocean
That seems known, then becomes a course
Bent on falling off the edge of your life.

What raised this wind to send you
Over the rollers of this ride?
Ten years old, maybe eleven
You think you're in some kind of heaven
Sitting between two of the cutest girls
That you have ever met. You can just bet
When you grow up, that you'll marry both.

Oh, look! Sinbad is in the rigging.
He whacks and hacks the many-headed monster.
There go two of the hairy tops! Nothing stops our hero.
The girls, what girls? Oh, the first married
A doctor went suburban.
The other sailed beyond a disappearing horizon.

No matter how well you may know the heavens,
The ocean's swells and currents may swiftly bring
You to a weed-clogged Sargasso Sea,
A nebulous destiny that leaves your sails
Listless; you thirst for a breeze.

You tack left, the waves push you right.
No land in sight, your charts refuse
To speak to you. Their clues to a safe haven
Are locked in ancient latitudes,
Longitudes and minus a few degrees.

Your craft rises and plunges in the gales.
You reach for remedies to tame the sea
That turns your gills a garish green.
You drop your anchors fore and aft.
Miracle to be told, they take hold.

You are near a half-familiar shore.
You load the ship's dinghy with brew and food,
Then bravely battle the flood to explore
The charted inlets of your life.

Spin Cycle

In laughter's terminal tug of war,
Death always grabs the last guffaw.
Our past dresses our bones
In its own fine spun cloth
To cover memories and nerves left raw.

We spend the present
Spin-drying in the every-day
Laundromat. Wrung out, we try to delay
The dwindling sun while waiting
For some future wind
To iron out our wrinkles.

What do they mean when they say,
"Going to get their hair done"?
Even interment straightens or curls
Scattered hirsute allure.

Pedicures merely provide
Short term temporal cures.
Nothing transient endures
Past the mortician's lipstick kiss
What we live signs our faces.
Little changes, though makeup makes it so

A Grave Plight

She loves me, perhaps too much,
Unguarded from the first green greeting;
A bit too forward to attract my heartbeat.
She stalked me even in my youth. I balked.
I wasn't prepared for a permanent promise.

I have to proffer the temptress her due.
She personifies sustained patience,
Defines subjective fidelity; and always
Essays to display her seductive phase.
She has this incorrigible cloying way.

One might comprehend how annoying
That can be, considering the source.
Perhaps others might not object, donning my shoes.
Given a chance, she would be omnipresent.

When I was young and feckless,
And by some accounts, a bit reckless,
We danced a heated tango that I couldn't endure.
After that, she wanted so much more.
I developed fleet feet, leaped fences
And bolted down back alley streets.

She never acted scorned and found dalliances
That catered to her fantastical whims
Between her relentless obsession with me.
Now that my hair is seasoned with salt,
My pace begins to slow to a halt.

At the threshold, she makes an appearance
To lure me past the safety of the door.
I wave her away and say "not yet".
She winks with a surety of the denouement.
Oh, Lady Death, will you still crave me
When I am bedded in the earth?
Will your love endure beyond the grave?

Peanut Butter

I borrowed the peanut butter
From your kitchen cabinet.
Two slices of Fiber +
Called to me from your
Refrigerator.
Your marshmallow fluff
Was tempting; but I refused
To be a cruel guest who would
Scrape the bottom of the jar;
So, I opened your fresh container
Of jam. I only took enough
From the top,
Just a little that you would not
Notice or miss.

More than that,
It returned me to my childhood,
To my parents' house not far
From the sound of the ocean.
My mind wandered back to those joys;
However, not long enough to get lost
In the past. Your bottle of pinot noir
Sang to me in a voice
That invited a symphony.
I longed to test the nose.
Thinking of the bouquet
That the label promised,
I regretted that I did not
Bring you an arrangement.
I passed no ATM on the way.
I knew that a five dollar bunch
Bought at the train station
Was beneath both of us.

Next time, I swear to bring roses
Which always conjure your image
In my thoughts.
Sadly, this moment, this day

Will turn to dust
As I must, too;
But, for now, I can only wonder
Where do you keep your
Seductive cork screw?

When Answers Chase Their Tails

Say that the ocean's murmuring voice
Reveals mysteries.
Say that the mountains leap
Or, do they tremble
When plates rattle on the shelf?
Say that the trees bow in reverence
Before the words of primal wind.
Say that death visits you in dreams.
Say that you refuse to take the first step
On the journey that never ends-
Except, you do when you first kick
And scream your entrance into life.
Say that you won't dance on graves
Of the wicked; although,
The temptation is strong.

Say that the world wobbles
Because humanity is out of balance.
Say that your design is righteous,
But you can't cure every wrong.
Say that the first step to heal
The planet is to plant a tree or seed.
One benevolent act begets another.
Say that you need to nurture your neighbor
Even if half the globe disagrees.
Say that mortal conflict creates new rivers.
When their waters recede back to their banks,
New gravestones raise their dripping heads
To inquire about the dead.

Say that life has many doors and knocks.
You're blameless half the time, with a little luck.
Don't get stuck in the muck with others' rebuke.
Say that you have options- except when you don't:
Roads with roses, paths with thorns. Sometimes both.
Say that they should select the door that hides the lady;
Avoid the tiger that grumbles on an empty stomach
And dreams of a full belly. You want the door on the right.

Radio Flyer

Cornered in your open nostalgic nook,
Surrounded by lamps, bric-a-brac and books,
Abandoned by a boy too soon grown to manhood,
Your engine-red body, your unbent wheels
Still pristine; rust on your handle
Reveals unpainted vintage.

Silent bells awaken memories;
To wonder why you were set aside.
Who would surrender the swift downhill ride?
Did you haul stacks of news papers
Door to door on a well-known route?
Were you a partner that carried the week's supplies

Bought at the neighborhood grocery store?
What feckless youth turned the page
When snow-tinted hair betrayed his age?
Many men revert to boys when they return
To such a priceless childhood joy.
Do you yearn for the one who treasured you last,

For your wheels to spin as fast as in your prime?
Now you dream, not quite alone,
In the shop of curios and reveries.
Soon another gleeful lad will appear
And claim you unequivocally as his own.
You will have a new home and a story that gleams.

Restoring the Bathroom Window

Gordian knots are undone,
Arduously, one by one.
The cord is released to raise the blind.
Opaque glass soon becomes as clear as an epiphany.
Vision surges unbound, internal and beyond
That which frames the interior world.

Chipped paint is methodically stripped.
Bare bone sill is massaged with sand paper.
A lavish coat leaves a clean sheen.
(Michelangelo, in my own mind.)
Next, the right side and the left
Receive the same transforming treatment.
The top is beyond my reach like more than a few
Elusive dreams. How it all gleams! A rebirth of space.

The wall bears a refurbished eye.
A window of possibility beckons.
Bathroom doors look a bit weary, forlorn.
Energy flows toward an expanded plan.
First the portals, then what's further in store
For this peerless Lazarus program?

Perhaps I can restore the color to autumn's
Crumbled leaves. No, that is not near my nascent skill.
Aha! Why not paint the sun dazzle at day's end?
Too late! It's already mounted on a canvas.

Twilight drains the vibrant spectrum.
Myriad stars gleam through the wall's one eye.
Where's my smock? There are no bounds
To what my brush might do;
However, a gallon of semi-gloss is not eternal.

Defining Fine Art

The canvas was clean, bare, barren,
Blank before framing the mass.
Darkness flowed from its surface;
So, He brushed away murky mise en scène
Until there was ample light for contrast.

Now, clear delineation unfolded.
A wet façade was introduced
As a base for ensuing texture.
So far, it was good but lacked color.
With a self-trained hand, landscape took shape.

A collage evolved with a complement of creatures.
Overhead, a medley of songbirds devised more depth
To this mural that spread on the horizon. Next, a sun
Flood to splash the entirety in shimmery veneer.
The accretion never ceased which rendered

The product with a muddy finish. From the morass,
He molded a biped and a mate. With all that weight,
The canvas cracked. Although the effort was
Reasonably sound, correct, the final picture-
Flawed, less than perfect. He vowed, at some point,
To revisit His venerated vision.

Spirit in a Bottle

"Then the Lord ...breathed into his nostrils
The breath of life; and man became a living soul."
Genesis 2:7

First, subtract the hair
That you comb daily.
It is merely a man's vanity.

Next, withdraw the eyes.
If they haven't seen doubtless proof,
Then, vision is absent.
Perhaps invisibility is the reason;
Or, just as likely, opaque disguise.

The nose is useless in this search.
What is sought has no scent;
Yet, incense inserts a hint
In temple refuge and church.

The mouth serves little purpose
In this quest—so, why propose?
Be sure to bottle the breath. Attach a label.
Affix your mark. Surrender the self.
Place within reach on a lower shelf.

Put the lungs in cold storage
For safe keeping; revisit later.
The heart might have been where
To start. Handle with crystal care.

Put the flesh in a cool cave.
Set the stage for future discovery.
The bones are next. The marrow
Should yield the meat of the matter;
However, it won't, at least not now.

Though the blood courses in passionate
Convolution, the solution is not there.
Sinews and muscles are red herrings.

Nothing to do but reassemble the parts.
Subtract the void; restore everything.
Rest assured that all are securely moored
To less than perfect memory.
Take down the bottle; remove the seal.
In a moment, the link will flow-don't blink.

Vacuum

Shall I compare her to Solomon?
She had her moments of wondrous wisdom.
Quick witted and even faster on her feet,
She kept pace with her jet-fueled progeny.

She wielded King David's shield to protect
The family from marauding storms.
She wore early widowhood like a crown.
Did she amass a treasure room of wealth?

She thought that her children were gems
Mined from the eyes of weeping angels.
Though she grieved two separate mates,
She found pleasure delving

Into fickle financial markets,
Sparing no remarks of
That Alice-In-Wonderland world.
Her opinions spanned the spectrum

In her efforts to understand
Shifting sands of a universe
That wobbled out of balance.
Now, her harvest droops in fallow field.

Grapes on the vine yield no wine.
There will be an empty chair on Passover.
Interred eleven fleeting years,
Tears have departed from the cup.

She converses silently in my dreams
And at daybreak's first gleaming.
Unheralded spirit comes and goes.
Memories, built of smiles, remain.

In a Spot

If you were a bathroom, where would you be?
Such a peculiar form of inquiry!
Still, I attest that query was rendered verbatim.
It is an arresting thought, a question that would stop
That train in the middle of a span.

Were I to venture an answer, I might reply,
Turn left, down the hall from the throne room
At Buckingham Palace. Or, perhaps you might find
The loo if you turn right past the servants' quarters
In a mansion facing the moors; or, seek le petit cabinet
As you pass the Masters' Exhibit on a Saturday at the Louvre.
The MOMA's docent may direct you; the MFA's security, for sure.
Any place like a swank hotel offers opportunity for relief
And release from worldly stress.

If I were a water closet, I would not want to be
An outhouse in winter's Northern Kingdom;
Nor, would I wish to be a powder room
In a solitary lighthouse in the North Sea.
Nor, would I want to be such a room of solitude

In the Moroccan Sahara; besides, it might only be a mirage.
A tough spot, to be in if nature calls.
If I were in that plight, I might not answer at all.

I'm not sure what other folks do, safe and secure
Ensconced upon the throne behind locked doors
Of their comfort rooms. Perhaps they clip coupons
Or check their stocks. Maybe they tend to the business
Of washing sweat-soaked socks,
Or texting friends, posting on face book.

Libraries often find their way to the loo.
It's not my business what others may do.
As for me, I contemplate mortality.
What inspirations, I shall not tell;
But, hidden away from a hard day's knocks,
I sense that it robustly surpasses
Plucking lint from my navel.

Name Tags

We are stacked sardines- no AC-
Packed, swimming in sweat
On the metro. Yet, more elbow
Through the wheezing door:
A rainbow tapestry of humanity.
Three are squeezed on either side
Of me, where, preferably two would
Fit more comfortably. Perhaps name
Tags would be fitting, for we are
Sitting in such close proximity.
"Hello, my name is... who are you?"
"Are you nobody, too?"

Negotiating for an Afterlife

How To Submit an Obit

The Flowing River accepts obituaries
Monday through Friday, nine to five.
Although there are no deadlines for the deceased,
The press has pressing schedules and matters.
Below, are some lively Heavenly hints.

The rumor of (full name here's) death is well-founded.
As he/ she moved forward to receive a just reward,
A plethora of family and friends surrounded
His/ her quiescent bed.

The decedent was known as a (fill in the blank) soul
Who enjoyed playing a charitable role.
He/ she will be missed,
Hopefully.

The deceased will be welcomed in the Beyond
By many proud antecedents
As well as a flock of ministering angels.
Here, you may list the departed's achievements, if any.
How do we measure the treasured deeds
Of a spirited life well-spent?

Services will be held at (name the address).
Unless decedent is cremated.
In lieu of flowers, please send chocolates.
He/ she so adored blessed sweets.
He/ she was often heard to proclaim
That they were simply heaven-sent treats.

Cemetery Visit

Years have passed since we've seen our father's stone.
It is so difficult to say goodbye.
I write, instead of visit, to atone.

In a sun-drizzled plot, he drifts alone.
His memory lives in every prayer I try.
Years have passed since we've seen our father's stone.

All our lives are merely on loan.
I rebel and demand to know why.
I write, rather than visit, to atone.

When grindstone struggle compels a groan,
I imagine his face in cloud framed sky.
Years have passed since we've seen our father's stone.

It's simple to observe that we are prone
To procrastinate when we should stop by.
I write, instead of visit, to atone.

In a dream, we spoke on the telephone;
Surprised to note that eyes remained dry.
Years have passed since we've seen our father's stone.
I write, instead of visit, to atone.

In Principio

"In the beginning was the Word."
Not that, what, or which one.
Nobody was there to hear;
So, any opinion ventured would be
Pure conjecture. Such an adventure,
To unravel that earliest mystery!

Myriad stories and histories were woven
Every era, both oral and written versions,
With facts chosen to fit each form. The formula,
Frequently a somewhat familiar recipe.
Many efforts ensued to perfect the norm.
With few primary resources, this became
An absurd pursuit, a blue ribbon exercise in futility.

Pyramids grew; clay tablets nearly caused a feud.
Empires rose and crumbled in search of the Word.
Crusades were fought in the name of the source.
The search marched with horns and banners,
All manner of alarms and arms in the name of revelation.
Spiritual journeys zig-zagged the horizon.
Seers and sages were imbued with visions.
Prophets rose and declined defining the WORD.

Word began with the, then expanded into dictionaries.
Veiled clues in those pages- perhaps hidden in plain view,
Surrounded by a surfeit of surreptitious suggestions.
Possibilities- many, probable- few, if any.
What word, so potent, could birth all creation?
An exhalation: Spirit, Man, back to Spirit.
Back to "In the beginning." Word may be sound.
Perhaps it is inside the aaah, or perhaps the Om;
Another option: seek it in the Amen.

Barbed Wire

We are fragile echoes and hovering memories
Of the old, young, and unborn who never
Lived to fulfill fated existence.
We once vibrantly trod the earth like you,
Your neighbor and itinerant stranger.
We used to weep, laugh, scream, and love.
Now, we are memorial voices.
Hear us, hear us, us, us!
Recite our Kaddish, you who dwell
In the world of transitory breath.
Jackboots violently stole our comprehending eyes,
Our gold and ivory tortured teeth,
Our prophetic words.
Dolorous wind wept as it performed
Its mournful task and carried away
Our chimney blasted funerary ashes.
We are the reluctant earth that nurtures
Death camps grieving flowers.
Our human elements ravenously consumed
By madman's stygian conflagration.
Gentle cosmos rescued martyred spirits.
You who have speech, strive to recite
Our histories. We are the Lord's
Lamented lesson. Learn, learn, learn!

Entreaty to the Trees*

1. Exhale, that we may breathe.

2. Spread your branches
   To shade and to shield.

3. Yield your limbs
   That we may sit or slumber.

4. Make a home for other creatures.

5. Blaze without fire
   In altered season.

6. Enlighten us
   In leaves dulcet discourse

7. Be watchful and pray
   Away the wooden ax handle.

8. Be a sentinel
   Over the living and dead.

9. Nourish with your full-blown fruit.

10. Bind the earth
    Before it bursts.

* Inspired by the Jewish Holiday for the Trees, *Tu B'Shvat*.

KOL

The voice is in the dulcet cello.
It flies from the chazzan's throat;
Sings in the words of our rabbi;
Calms trembling hearts of devout defendants.

It is a great, elated voice;
A soft, comforting tone;
An invitation, if needed,
A gentle prompt for us to note
Where we are, and where we shall be.

The voice is in the shofar's alarm,
A sound of grief, joy, and absolution;
A call to teshuva and resolution.
Our contrite cry is palpable.
Penitent prayers may purchase reprieve.
We are ready to heed the voice that heals.

The voice is in the curtained ark;
Yet the cadence surrounds,
Hovers, remote and near;
Whispers in our ears.
The voice flows over reverent throngs.
It is neither lonely nor alone.

Special Delivery

Dear Whatever-You-Are,
Yes, I know some time has flowed past.
A lot of mundane cares prevented me
From keeping more in touch since our last
Discourse. Sometimes the world is too much with me;
However, spring has finally delivered its cheer.

Birds trill their own hallelujah chorus
And have had sundry conversations to sort
Out claims on private domains.

Garden flora are already arrayed in sunny-day finery,
Sing hosannas to glorious rays.
The lake mirrors sky forms hurrying on myriad errands.
They sometimes stop to drift in contemplation.
No doubt, the landscaped terraces beyond the veil
Are beyond the scale of this frail world.

You most likely know that you are always
In my reflections and ever-present prayers.
This letter will be sent via Heaven Express,
Wending through layers that limit my vision.

Sometimes sight is better looking within.
My heart is 20/20; my eyes' clarity continues to improve.
I am a vintage bottle with gradual aging.
As I labor in the vineyards, daily travails vanish;
Lacy mists, sundered by laser sun, transform
To dazzling dewdrops that anoint the grass.

I chant solos of thanks for blessings, major and minute.
The wind's soft notes are an accompanying flute.
Thanks be to you for each added day of breath
As Nature's perfumed bounty permeates the air.

This missive increases with its recitation.
Perhaps I should cease my documentation
Before it is treated as tedious mail.

Please check your directory and look up my folks;
Let them know they're in my constant memories
And prayers. It would be nice for them to visit a bit more,
Even though it would be only in my pre-dawn dreams.

Softer Than Silence

Hear my loud silence, oh Lord!
At its center is the small cry.
Beneath its layers, find my prayer.

The chazzan has a voice
That soars to the world's roof.
My rabbi's chants are like paired
Pianos playing Mendelssohn,
Wisdom crowns her knowing air.

An aperture is in my heart.
Part is opaque; the other, clear.
 Sometimes, the voice takes refuge there
To impart inscrutable wonders.

Sometimes, it reigns in reticence.
It has that right when one peers in.
Often, the best advice is none.
In mute amazement, the voice sprouts ears
To hear questions in the percussion.

Answers grow wings in stillness.
The window only needs to be slightly ajar,
And the replies fly out
To cohere with unfettered prayer.

Spirit Tree
For Kaji Aso

I went to the Public Gardens to seek release.
Relentless stress mocks every waking hour.
A wise teacher lives there in the symbol of a tree.
A message from him to me would free my coiled mind.
Alive, he was the centered artist, I the ardent student.
His energy gave others creative power.

To meditate, to meet again.
I grip the sentient branch in greeting,
A bond between two planes of being.
Hello, Mr. Aso, I am here.
I presume that you are there.

Clouds dress the sun in scarlet robes.
The spirit tree of memory
Is rooted in a circle of serenity.
I listen for the words, the answers.
In the silence, I understand.

Behind me, the Ether Fountain speaks
In a half-known voice. Floating lights
Cast soft tones. Soon mirrored stars
Will bathe the leafy sentinel in pulsating night.

Stopping by the Shul
After Robert Frost

Whose shul, this is, I think I know.
His home is in the shtetl, though.
He will not see me stopping here
To offer up most solemn prayer
At, perhaps, the holiest time of year.
He would wonder what hidden mistake
Would make my words quiver and my knees quake
As I daven near calm and reflecting lake.
New mitzvahs are vowed to heal the earth;
To show clear evidence of our worth;
A chance for cleansing and future mirth.
The ram's horn voice is rich and deep.
I am weary, the way is steep;
But there are pledges to God and Man to keep.

Among Us

The breeze stretches pliant forms,
Kinetic art, brush-stroked clouds.
There, profiles in near bas-relief;
Here, a giant in repose.
And there, so close, you can almost
Reach up to pluck a feather,
A perfect pair of sculpted wings,
A flaming figure in the middle.
An Arch-Angel over Boston.

Senses soar toward the sun
When rays sear through languid clouds,
Revealing noble haloed heads.
Perhaps when we look for them,
We can see angels everywhere.
Be careful whom you tell.

Directions

First, gather the ovened potatoes;
Then, strip away earth-toned skin.
Next, mash them beyond recognition
Of their former, somewhat oval, contour.
Pile up snow white mound on the counter
Or place on the vintage kitchen table.

Walk away from the mass and return
To gain new insight. Tell yourself that
What remains has profound meaning.
Continue to shape it into a lunar landscape.

Shortly, you encounter a senior moment;
So, you turn to God for enlightenment.
You wait for a late-arriving answer.
For some reason, you still listen,
Anticipating the postponed response.

I-F

You wrote a reality check today.
It came back stamped insufficient funds.
The New Year redeems dog-eared coupons.
Dust drifts on your mind's shelves.
Cluttered space awaits the next delivery.

What ifs gurgle down the drain
Of rusted possibilities.
Lists cinder through synapses,
Flutter on memory's breeze.
Images machete through invasive weeds.

You slap mortar between the bricks.
The tide pushes past your thumb.
You hold your breath while the tsunami
Towers and twists like an ocean-spawned bull.

You strive to shackle demonic storms.
Waves' arms reach to rip you loose.
Your account holds, the roof is strong.
The wind chants its chorus to the siren's song.

Butt

She ignites the head
Of a dead cigarette.
I turn the tarot card,
In turmoil, I look away.
What warning can you say
That hasn't already been said
To one with such a fateful need?

The lethal light welcomes
Night. Stars look away.
A book, a butt, a room,
Sleep keeps a death watch.
The smoldering ash grows,
Then droops.

Eye lids are in a futile fight.
A flicker blossoms in full bloom.
Tendrils ascend the walls of the room.
The book is an adventure tome.

Eyes close, mimic living pose.
The loom stops; one of three
Severs measured thread.
She is only sixteen; but, there are the butts.
Searing smoke fumes linger.

Peak of Promise

1.
On that peak, an ark teetered-
Civilization in an awkward balance.

On that mountain, the fire giver, chained,
Maimed by merciless beak of regal bird.

On that mountain, the Word, first heard.
Then, fury furthered the absurd.

Sanctified tablets shattered;
Holy writ reduced to clay shards.

On that mountain, the final clangor
Of fulgent light and swarming darkness.

On that peak, baying carnivores,
Heralds of the four feared horsemen.

2.
Pile minute molehill upon molehill.
Ultimately, you may get a mountain.

Explode a mountain and you may uncover
Molehills stirred into mere remnants and rubble.

That hill once had a higher, eminent peak.
Seekers of solitude would discover voices

Of wolves singing their keening songs.
Now, machines have devoured the summit.

Strive to ascend that sacred mountain-
No, definitely not that one.

The mount that you seek has a peak
That lets you peer down to a pristine valley.

Your trek is guiding you closer.
Look inward. Yes, that one!

Hold It

Say you stop breathing for just a moment or two.
It's different than the norm, especially for you.
Perhaps you're merely trying to catch and hold a breath.
Could be that your heart and lungs are deciding
Whether to continue. Maybe arrest will suffice
To pump enough air to jump-start you to another plane.
How do you measure if you inherit a molecule or two,
Expelled in a teardrop, laughter, prayer?

Whose minute puff mingles with yours?
Perhaps it migrated from a disintegrated Pope,
A High Priest, or Rabbi; a Christian, Muslim, or Jew.
Might be from a prince, a queen, beggar, conman,
Alexander, Caesar, Barabbas, Genghis Khan,
Napoleon, a foot soldier, an ordinary citizen;
Maybe all of these swarming like bees.

How many generations exhaled their last
And sent a bottle's worth tumbling down line to you?
From grandfather to the nth power or perhaps
Grandmother times twelve removed from this sphere.
Whose merged with yours; at what moment did each
Micro event occur? Did you note it? Did you keep
A written record for future heirs?
Each infinitesimal space, born of laughter, tears,
A whisper, a prayer. Unbreakable links connect
This legacy. When your heart inscribes its big bang fact,
Who will inherit the mite's breath,
That part of you that is all your parts?

The Day After My Death

"Imagining what the weather will be like
On the day following your death…"
From "Helium by Billy Collins

The day after my death,
Clouds will cease their teardrops flow.
The sky will take a deep breath,
Then exhale, hustling drifting forms
That may have hesitated a bit
To pose for human eyes.

A riderless Pegasus shape-shifts
To a gazelle pursued by a dissolving dragon.
Dispersing clouds diminish growing faces.
Why are there no angels floating past?

The day after my death,
The sun will rehearse its optimistic glow.
Darkling palls may come and go;
But each tomorrow hopefully
Improves over the previous twenty-four.

If the day after my demise
Falls on a January date
Interment may await spring advent
When the Earth is busy with rebirth.
Snow can interfere with the best intent.

The day after my death,
Markets may rise or decline
Without any comments from me.
My opinions have limited current effect.
Commerce will motor on with uneven
Bottom lines unaltered by
The closing of my account.

The day after my death,
Earth will lumber along
Licking its wounds, working
To recover from its own
Long, miasmic malaise.

The day after my death,
My soul may choose to linger
Thirty-nine more to subtly tie up
Loosened ends; to make the rounds
For missed farewells. It's never too late
For mending fences.
I'll knock three times to signal
My presence. I won't be offended
If you choose not to reply.

About the Author

Harris Gardner has been the Poetry Editor of Ibbetson Street since 2010. He has authored four poetry collections: *Chalice of Eros*, co-authored with Lainie Senechal (Stone Soup Press) 1998; *Lest They Become* (Ibbetson Street Press) 2003; *Among Us* (Červená Barva Press) 2007; *No Time for Death* (Červená Barva Press) 2022. His numerous publication credits include *The Harvard Review*, *A Poet's Siddur*, *Midstream*, *Cool Plums*, *Rosebud*, *Fulcrum*, *Chest*, *The Aurorean*, Ibbetson street, Constellations (#6 and #7), Main Street Rag, *Vallum* (Canada), *Levure Littéraire* (France), *Green Door* (Belgium), *Muddy River Poetry Review*, *Wilderness House Literary Review*, *The Jewish Advocate*, *The New Renaissance*, *Endicott Review*, *Concrete Wolf*, *I Refused to Die* (A Holocaust Anthology of stories of Boston Area Holocaust Survivors and Soldiers Who Liberated the Concentration Camps of World War II), *Bagels with the Bards Anthology*, *Merrimac Mic Anthology*, and others.

He co-founded, with Lainie Senechal, Tapestry of Voices, 1999 to the present); Co-founded, with Lainie Senechal, The Boston National Poetry Month Festival, 2001 to the present; Co-founded, with Doug Holder (his brainchild) Breaking Bagels with the Bards, 2005 to the present. Gardner was Poet-in-Residence at Endicott College, 2002- April, 2005. He founded and hosted many poetry venues over the past twenty-two years, a few which ran simultaneously for up to eight years including Boston Borders, Poetry in The Chapel Series (Forest Hills Cemetery), Mad Poets Café (Pawtucket, R.I.); others included The Parker House Hotel, The Laureate Series at Boston City Hall, and, currently, The First and Last Word Poetry Series, Co-founded and co-hosted with Gloria Mindock, 2010 to the present. He has been featured at many venues in New England.

He has been a member of six blue ribbon Poet Laureate selection committees: three for Boston and three for Somerville. His poetry has been nominated for two Pushcart Prizes and he received honorable mention for the New England Poetry Club's Boyle-Farber Prize. In 2015, he received a Life Time Achievement Award from Ibbetson Street Press and a Citation from the Massachusetts House of Representatives.

He is currently a member of the Academy of American Poets.